THE BLACK SATURDAY

A book that tells the story of October 7th, the day that became known as Black Saturday.

Inspired by Trey yingst

William L. Jorgenson

Copyright Page

Why is Trey Yingst's account of October 7th significant? Trey Yingst's on-the-ground reporting brought a human element to the global audience, making the conflict more understandable and relatable to people worldwide. His experience as a journalist gave his narrative authenticity and depth.

How did the events of October 7th affect international relations? The aftermath of October 7th saw shifts in diplomatic relations, with countries re-evaluating their alliances, policies, and humanitarian responsibilities. It also sparked conversations on the role of media in conflicts.

What are the challenges of reporting in conflict zones like October 7th? Journalists face immense danger, emotional strain, and ethical dilemmas when covering conflicts. Maintaining objectivity while ensuring accurate and timely reporting is a challenge in such volatile situations.

What legacy did Trey Yingst leave after reporting on October 7th? Trey Yingst solidified his reputation as one of the most courageous war correspondents of his generation. His legacy lies in his commitment to showing the truth, no matter how difficult or dangerous it may be.

TABLE OF CONTENT

THE CALM BEFORE THE STORM 9

    Geopolitical Landscape Pre-October 7th............................9

    Regional Tensions 9

    Historical Conflicts 11

    Trey Yingst's Early Life and Career 12

    How He Became a War Correspondent............................14

    His Experiences in Other Conflict Zones..........................16

THE BREAKING POINT—OCTOBER 7TH...19

    Timeline of Events 19

    Early Morning: First Signs of Conflict..............................19

    Mid-Day Developments...22

    The Eyewitness Report 24

    Trey Yingst's Coverage of the Events 27

    Key Interviews and Reports from the Ground 27

THE HUMAN ELEMENT—SURVIVORS AND VICTIMS 31

    Stories of Survival 31

    Personal Accounts from Those Affected 32

    The Human Toll of the Conflict..36

    Emotional Toll on Journalists...38

    The Psychological Impact on Trey Yingst........................42

    The Burden of Reporting in Real-Time 44

THE GLOBAL REACTION 47

How the World Responded to October 7th 47

Political Reactions...48

Media Coverage from Different Regions.....................................52

The Impact on International Relations 55

Diplomatic Consequences 59

Long-Term Changes in Policy..62

THE AFTERMATH—A CHANGED LANDSCAPE 67

Efforts to Rebuild Post-Conflict 67

Reconciliation and Healing 70

The Role of the International Community.....................................72

The Legacy of October 7th 74

Humanitarian Response to the Crisis 75

How Trey Yingst Reflected on the Events.....................................77

His Post-Conflict Coverage 81

Long-Term Impact on His Career...82

THE POWER OF JOURNALISM IN CONFLICT ZONES 85

The Role of War Correspondents 85

How Journalists Shape the Narrative 86

Ethical Dilemmas in Reporting 88

Trey Yingst's Legacy as a Journalist 89

His Unique Approach to Storytelling 92

The Impact of His Reports on the Global Audience 93

CONCLUSION 97

Reflecting on "The Saturday That Turned Black" 97

Lessons Learned from October 7th 98

The Continued Importance of Journalism in Crisis Reporting........99

THE CALM BEFORE THE STORM

Geopolitical Landscape Pre-October 7th

The events leading up to October 7th did not occur in isolation; they were the result of complex and long-standing geopolitical tensions. The region had been a hotbed of conflict, with various political factions and foreign powers vying for control, influence, and resources. Years of unresolved disputes, deep-seated grievances, and historical territorial conflicts created an environment where violence was always simmering beneath the surface. These underlying tensions became the catalyst for the fateful day.

Regional Tensions

At the heart of the conflict were age-old territorial disputes that had defined relationships between neighboring countries for decades. These disputes often revolved around contested borders, access to key resources like water, and religious and ethnic divisions that stretched back generations. Several peace agreements had been brokered in the past, but they were fragile, often collapsing under the weight of mistrust and sporadic violence.

In addition to these local disputes, the region was heavily influenced by the involvement of larger global powers. These powers had their own strategic interests, backing different sides of the conflict, which only added fuel to the fire. The local population was caught between powerful political and military interests, with many civilians living under the constant threat of violence or displacement. Despite occasional periods of calm, tensions were always high, and both the people and the governments knew that another major conflict was only a matter of time.

As October 7th approached, the atmosphere became more charged. Diplomatic efforts had begun to falter, with talks between key players breaking down. Military activity started to increase along the borders, and rumors of an impending escalation spread quickly. Yet, to many, this seemed like another cycle of tensions that would soon dissipate as had happened before. However, this time, things would be different. The calm that settled over the region was deceptive, hiding the brewing storm that was about to explode in full force.

Historical Conflicts

The region's history was marked by a series of protracted conflicts that shaped its modern-day political landscape. Many of these historical conflicts were rooted in colonial legacies, religious differences, and ethnic divisions that had festered for centuries. Key players in the region had long-standing grievances, often over territorial boundaries drawn without regard for the cultural and tribal affiliations of the people living there. This created a volatile situation where alliances shifted frequently, and violence was a constant threat.

Over the decades, several wars had erupted between neighboring nations, often ignited by territorial disputes or struggles for political dominance. These conflicts left behind scars, both physical and psychological, as entire cities were destroyed, and countless lives were lost. The presence of foreign intervention further complicated the situation, with global powers backing different sides, driven by their own strategic interests.

The outcomes of these conflicts were often inconclusive, leading to ceasefires that were shaky at best. While peace agreements were sometimes reached, they rarely addressed the underlying issues that sparked the violence in the first place. Instead, they acted as temporary band-aids on a much deeper wound. This history of unresolved conflict created an atmosphere of distrust and fear, where people lived under the constant threat of renewed fighting.

By the time October 7th arrived, the weight of this history hung heavy over the region. The events of that day were not just about the immediate conflict—they were the culmination of decades, even centuries, of unresolved tensions, with many seeing it as a tragic but inevitable consequence of the region's troubled past.

Trey Yingst's Early Life and Career

Trey Yingst, born and raised in the United States, had always been driven by a passion for uncovering the truth and telling stories that mattered. From a young age, he was drawn to the world of journalism, particularly the kind of reporting that brought attention to underreported conflicts and crises. His determination to become a voice for those who often went unheard led him to pursue a degree in broadcast journalism, where he honed his skills in storytelling, investigative research, and live reporting.

Yingst's career began in the U.S., where he covered local and national stories for various news outlets. However, it wasn't long before he realized that his true calling was international reporting. The world's most dangerous and conflict-ridden zones became his beat, as he sought to shed light on the human cost of war and political instability. His ability to report from some of the most volatile regions of the world quickly gained him recognition.

His fearless approach to journalism took him to the frontlines of many major global conflicts. From covering civil wars to reporting on the humanitarian crises that followed, Yingst was relentless in his pursuit of the truth. He believed in showing the world the raw, unfiltered realities of war, and his work often highlighted the voices of those directly affected—civilians, refugees, and victims of violence.

Over the years, Yingst became known not just for his in-depth reporting, but for his ability to stay composed in the face of extreme danger. His dedication to his craft and his commitment to truth-telling earned him a reputation as one of the most respected war correspondents of his generation. His work on the ground, especially during moments of crisis like October 7th, has had a lasting impact on how global audiences perceive conflict zones and the lives of those caught in the crossfire.

By the time the events of "The Saturday That Turned Black" unfolded, Yingst had already established himself as a fearless journalist, one who was unafraid to stand in the middle of chaos to deliver the truth to the world. His early life and career set the foundation for the kind of reporter he became—one who brought a sense of humanity to stories that often seemed distant and impersonal.

How He Became a War Correspondent

Trey Yingst's path to becoming a war correspondent wasn't planned from the start, but his passion for journalism and truth-telling naturally led him to that role. After studying broadcast journalism in college, he began his career covering local stories and national news in the United States. While these stories were important, he quickly realized that his true interest lay in international affairs, particularly in regions affected by conflict. He wanted to tell the stories that others were either unable or unwilling to cover.

Yingst's determination to bring attention to underreported crises drove him to take bold steps early in his career. While many journalists start with safer assignments, he sought out opportunities to report from conflict zones, knowing that these stories were critical but often overlooked by mainstream media. His first big break came when he began working for News2Share, an independent media outlet that focused on global conflicts and political movements. This gave him the platform to report from areas many journalists avoided due to the dangers involved.

His early work covering protests, riots, and conflicts in various regions earned him recognition as a courageous reporter. He was not just reporting from a distance but was often in the middle of the action, delivering live updates as events unfolded. This on-the-ground experience helped Yingst build the skills needed to work in war zones—quick thinking, risk management, and, most importantly, a deep sense of empathy for the people he was reporting on.

As he gained more experience, major news networks took notice. Eventually, Yingst joined Fox News, which gave him the resources and platform to report from some of the most dangerous places in the world. His willingness to be on the frontlines, no matter the risk, quickly solidified his reputation as a dedicated war correspondent. His career trajectory was marked by his relentless pursuit of the truth, no matter how difficult or dangerous the environment.

His Experiences in Other Conflict Zones

Before covering the events of October 7th, Trey Yingst had already built an extensive portfolio of work from various conflict zones around the world. His experience spanned multiple regions, each with its own unique challenges and dangers.

One of the first major conflicts Yingst covered was the Israeli-Palestinian conflict. Reporting from the Gaza Strip and other volatile areas, he witnessed firsthand the devastating effects of years of ongoing violence. His work from Gaza included live coverage during airstrikes, documenting the immediate impact on civilians. These experiences not only tested his ability to report under extreme pressure but also deepened his understanding of the human cost of war.

Yingst also reported from Syria, another war-torn region where violence and chaos had displaced millions of people. His coverage of the Syrian civil war brought attention to the refugee crisis and the struggles of those trying to escape the conflict. Reporting from the frontlines, he gave a voice to those suffering in silence, highlighting their stories of survival and resilience. Syria was a particularly dangerous assignment, with shifting frontlines and multiple factions involved, but Yingst's reporting helped the world see the complexities of the conflict beyond the headlines.

In addition to the Middle East, Yingst covered conflicts in Africa, including the war in Ethiopia and political instability in countries like South Sudan. His work from these regions highlighted the widespread effects of civil unrest and governmental collapse, often focusing on how civilians, especially women and children, were disproportionately affected by the violence.

In all these conflict zones, Yingst brought a human face to the stories, focusing on the lives impacted by war and violence rather than just the political and military aspects. His ability to connect with people on the ground and share their experiences with the world made his reporting deeply impactful. These experiences shaped Yingst into the journalist he is today, one who understands that the true cost of conflict is often borne by those far removed from the decision-makers.

By the time he reported on the events of October 7th, Trey Yingst had already earned a reputation as a seasoned war correspondent, capable of delivering compelling, human-focused stories from some of the most dangerous places in the world. His previous experiences in other conflict zones gave him the expertise and resilience needed to navigate the chaos and devastation of that fateful day.

THE BREAKING POINT—OCTOBER 7TH

Timeline of Events

The events of October 7th unfolded with a chilling rapidity, transforming what began as a seemingly quiet day into a historic turning point. The escalation of violence was swift, leaving little time for those on the ground to react, and the world watched in shock as the situation spiraled out of control. Trey Yingst, stationed in the region, was one of the first journalists to report live as the crisis began to unfold, offering an eyewitness account of each moment as it happened.

Early Morning: First Signs of Conflict

In the early hours of October 7th, the region was calm, though there had been underlying tensions for days. Local residents, journalists, and officials all had the sense that something was brewing, but the specific trigger for conflict remained unclear. At dawn, the first signs of trouble appeared in the form of unexpected military movements. Trey Yingst, already in position for what was expected to be a routine day of reporting, began noticing an increase in troop activity along key border areas. This was the first indication that something was amiss.

Around 6:00 AM, intelligence reports started to surface, indicating a heightened risk of an imminent attack. The atmosphere became tense as security forces were placed on high alert. Residents in nearby towns, who had been accustomed to periodic warnings, began to notice increased patrols and checkpoints. Rumors circulated quickly through local networks, with conflicting reports about the scale and seriousness of the situation.

As the morning wore on, the first explosions were heard. These initial blasts were faint, distant enough that many people dismissed them as routine military drills or isolated skirmishes. But as the minutes passed, the sounds of conflict grew louder and more persistent. By 7:00 AM, it was clear to Trey Yingst and others on the ground that this was no ordinary event. Something far more significant was happening.

By 8:00 AM, the situation had escalated into a full-blown conflict. Artillery fire and airstrikes began hitting key locations, and the intensity of the violence rapidly increased. Civilians scrambled for cover as warnings to take shelter blared through loudspeakers in urban centers. Roads were quickly closed off, and emergency services were overwhelmed by the initial casualties.

For Trey Yingst, this was the beginning of what would become one of the most intense days of his career. As the situation deteriorated, he set up his reporting equipment, ready to broadcast live updates to a global audience. His early morning reports captured the confusion, fear, and rising panic as the scale of the conflict began to take shape. His voice, calm but tense, narrated the unfolding chaos, providing a real-time account of the events that would soon grip the world's attention.

The early morning hours of October 7th were a tipping point, a moment when the fragile peace in the region shattered, and the world began to witness a conflict that would leave lasting scars. Those first few hours were crucial in setting the tone for what was to come, as the situation rapidly escalated beyond anyone's control.

Mid-Day Developments

By mid-day on October 7th, the situation had devolved into chaos, with fighting spreading across the region. What began as isolated incidents escalated into widespread violence, engulfing entire neighborhoods and cities. Trey Yingst, positioned in a strategic location to observe the unfolding events, provided a relentless stream of updates, detailing the harrowing developments as they occurred.

Around noon, the number of explosions increased dramatically. Airstrikes targeted various areas, including civilian infrastructure and military installations. Eyewitness accounts began flooding in from locals who were trapped in the middle of the conflict. These reports painted a grim picture of the situation, revealing the devastating impact on families and communities. Homes were destroyed, and many people were left injured or dead as the fighting intensified.

As Yingst broadcast live, he described the scenes of devastation around him. He narrated stories of families who had been torn apart by the violence and showed footage of emergency services trying to rescue the injured. The sights and sounds of war became increasingly overwhelming, and the urgency in his voice reflected the gravity of the moment.

People fled from their homes, seeking safety in makeshift shelters or crowded public areas, but chaos ensued as panic spread. Streets that were once bustling with life were now filled with debris and fear. Eyewitnesses recounted tales of harrowing escapes, while others stood frozen, unsure of what to do next.

In addition to the immediate violence, the humanitarian crisis began to unfold. Aid organizations reported that they were unable to reach those in need due to the dangerous conditions on the ground. As Yingst reported on these developments, he emphasized the importance of international attention and support. He called for humanitarian access to the affected areas, urging viewers to understand that behind every statistic was a real person suffering.

Yingst's mid-day reports captured the desperation and heartbreak of those caught in the conflict. He highlighted the resilience of local communities, sharing stories of individuals who bravely stepped up to help their neighbors, often risking their own safety in the process. These moments of human kindness amidst chaos offered a glimmer of hope, reminding audiences that even in the darkest of times, humanity could prevail.

The mid-day developments of October 7th served as a turning point, transforming the conflict from a series of isolated incidents into a full-blown humanitarian crisis. The world began to take notice, and the urgency of the situation became clear, setting the stage for the days and weeks to follow.

The Eyewitness Report

Trey Yingst's eyewitness report from the frontlines of October 7th became a vital source of information for viewers worldwide. As a seasoned war correspondent, he understood the responsibility he carried to accurately portray the events while also honoring the lives affected by the violence. His approach was rooted in compassion, and his reporting aimed to connect audiences with the human experiences behind the headlines.

From the very beginning of his coverage, Yingst established a rapport with his audience, often addressing them directly as if they were there with him. "This isn't just a story," he would say, "these are real people facing unimaginable challenges." His narrative style, which combined factual reporting with poignant storytelling, drew viewers in, compelling them to pay attention to the suffering occurring in real-time.

24

Throughout his live broadcasts, Yingst provided a detailed account of the violence surrounding him. He shared the sights and sounds that filled the air—the wailing of sirens, the distant thuds of explosions, and the cries of those in distress. He painted a vivid picture of the scene, describing the chaos in the streets, the terrified expressions on people's faces, and the urgency of rescue efforts.

He often introduced viewers to individuals whose lives had been irrevocably changed that day. One notable segment featured a mother who had lost her child in the violence. Yingst interviewed her on camera, allowing her to share her story, her grief palpable. "This is the human cost of conflict," he stated, underscoring the importance of putting faces to the numbers reported in the media.

Yingst's report was not only a recounting of the day's events; it was a call to action. He emphasized the need for humanitarian aid and international support, urging viewers to understand the severity of the situation. His powerful messaging resonated, highlighting that the conflict was not merely a distant issue but one that demanded attention and empathy from a global audience.

As the day wore on and the situation continued to evolve, Yingst remained a steadfast presence on the ground. He kept his camera rolling, capturing the unfolding drama while providing context and analysis. His commitment to reporting the truth, despite the chaos and danger surrounding him, solidified his reputation as a dedicated journalist who truly understood the weight of his words.

The eyewitness report from October 7th became a significant part of Yingst's legacy as a war correspondent. It illustrated the real and immediate impact of conflict on human lives, serving as a reminder of the importance of compassionate reporting in times of crisis. Through his lens, viewers witnessed the horror of war, but they also saw resilience, courage, and the enduring spirit of those affected by the violence.

Trey Yingst's Coverage of the Events

As the chaos of October 7th unfolded, Trey Yingst's presence on the ground became a lifeline for viewers seeking to understand the gravity of the situation. His unwavering commitment to delivering accurate and compassionate reporting stood out amidst the cacophony of violence. Through a series of live broadcasts and key interviews, Yingst captured the stark reality of the conflict, ensuring that the human stories behind the headlines were not lost.

One of the most powerful aspects of Yingst's coverage was his ability to connect with individuals directly affected by the violence. He sought out civilians, humanitarian workers, and local officials, eager to share their experiences and perspectives with the world. Each interview provided a unique glimpse into the heart of the crisis, revealing the multifaceted impact of the conflict on daily life.

Key Interviews and Reports from the Ground
Interview with a Local Doctor

One of the most poignant interviews Yingst conducted was with a local doctor who had just returned from a makeshift hospital. The doctor described the overwhelming influx of injured civilians, many suffering from blast wounds and shrapnel injuries. "We are doing everything we can, but the resources are limited," he explained, his voice strained with exhaustion. "We need more medical supplies and support."

This interview highlighted the urgent humanitarian crisis that was unfolding, emphasizing the need for immediate assistance from the international community. Yingst's presentation of the doctor's plea resonated with viewers, sparking discussions about how individuals could contribute to relief efforts.

Testimony of a Displaced Family
In another moving segment, Yingst met a family who had fled their home as the fighting escalated. The parents recounted their harrowing escape, describing how they had to leave behind everything they owned. "We ran with our children, not knowing if we would make it out alive," the father said, tears in his eyes. "All we wanted was safety."

Yingst's respectful and empathetic approach allowed the family to share their story authentically, making the crisis feel personal and relatable to viewers. The interview was a powerful reminder of the human toll of war, illustrating how quickly lives can be upended.

Reports on Humanitarian Efforts

Yingst also reported on the tireless work of humanitarian organizations trying to provide aid in the midst of chaos. He visited relief centers that had opened to assist displaced families, showcasing the efforts of volunteers who were distributing food, water, and medical supplies. "Even in the face of destruction, there are people fighting to help one another," Yingst remarked, highlighting the resilience of the human spirit amid despair.

These reports painted a broader picture of the crisis, illustrating that while violence dominated the headlines, there were still stories of hope and community solidarity. Yingst's coverage of these humanitarian efforts served as a call to action for those watching, encouraging support for organizations working on the ground.

Government and Military Perspectives

To provide a comprehensive view of the unfolding situation, Yingst also sought out local officials and military representatives for interviews. These discussions were often fraught with tension, as officials offered differing perspectives on the conflict's origins and developments. "We are taking necessary measures to protect our citizens," a military spokesperson stated during one broadcast. "But we need the world to understand the complexities of our situation."

While these interviews added depth to Yingst's reporting, they also underscored the often conflicting narratives that emerged during such crises. By presenting various viewpoints, Yingst aimed to inform his audience while emphasizing the need for nuanced understanding in the face of conflict.

Through these key interviews and reports, Trey Yingst captured the essence of the events of October 7th, offering a human-centered narrative that transcended mere statistics. His ability to connect with individuals and share their stories underscored the profound impact of the crisis, ensuring that the voices of those affected were heard loud and clear in a world often desensitized to the realities of war. Yingst's coverage became not just a record of events, but a testament to the strength and resilience of the human spirit amid tragedy.

THE HUMAN ELEMENT—SURVIVORS AND VICTIMS

Stories of Survival

Amid the chaos and devastation of October 7th, the stories of survival emerged as a testament to the resilience of the human spirit. Each account from those who lived through the harrowing events served as a poignant reminder of the strength and courage found in the most desperate circumstances. Trey Yingst's coverage included not only the stark realities of violence but also the inspiring tales of individuals who managed to escape and adapt amidst the turmoil.

These stories of survival highlight the determination of ordinary people who faced extraordinary challenges, showcasing their will to live, protect their loved ones, and rebuild their lives despite overwhelming odds. As Yingst reported, these narratives brought a human face to the tragedy, emphasizing that behind every statistic was a story waiting to be told.

Personal Accounts from Those Affected

A Father's Determination

One of the most moving personal accounts came from a father named Amir, who recounted the harrowing day when he had to make a split-second decision to protect his children. As the explosions began, Amir gathered his family, urging them to leave their home. "I could hear the blasts getting closer, and all I could think about was getting my kids to safety," he shared, his voice trembling with emotion.

Amir described their frantic escape through the streets, dodging debris and chaos. They eventually found shelter in a local community center, where families were gathering for safety. "It was terrifying, but we made it," he said, a glimmer of hope in his eyes. His story resonated with many, illustrating the lengths to which a parent will go to ensure their children's safety.

The Courage of a Young Girl

Another powerful account came from a young girl named Layla, who, despite her tender age, displayed remarkable bravery. Layla was playing in her yard when the conflict erupted. "At first, I didn't understand what was happening," she said, her eyes wide with innocence. "But when I saw the sky filled with smoke, I ran inside to find my mom."

In the midst of chaos, Layla's quick thinking helped her family escape. She led her mother and younger siblings to a nearby building that had become a makeshift shelter for those fleeing the violence. "I just knew we had to go somewhere safe," Layla recounted, proud of her ability to keep her family together during such a frightening time.

Her story became a symbol of hope for many, as it highlighted the resilience and courage that can emerge even in the youngest of individuals during a crisis.

A Community's Response

Survivors often spoke not only of their personal struggles but also of the collective strength of their community. In the aftermath of the violence, local residents banded together to support one another. Maria, a local shop owner, opened her doors to those in need, providing food and water to families who had lost everything. "We are all in this together," she emphasized. "If we don't help each other, who will?"

Maria's story illustrated the profound sense of solidarity that can arise in the face of adversity. Her actions inspired many, proving that kindness and compassion can shine through even the darkest moments.

The Aftermath of Loss

However, not all accounts were filled with hope. Many survivors also shared the pain of loss and the challenges they faced in rebuilding their lives. Ahmed, a teacher who lost several friends in the violence, reflected on the emotional toll of the events. "I can't forget what happened that day," he admitted. "Every time I close my eyes, I see the faces of those we lost."

Despite his grief, Ahmed also emphasized the importance of remembrance and resilience. "We must honor their memories by rebuilding our community," he stated, embodying the spirit of perseverance that characterized so many accounts.

Seeking Justice and Healing

The aftermath of the conflict left many survivors grappling with trauma and seeking justice. Layla's mother, who had lost her husband in the violence, spoke about the need for accountability. "We must hold those responsible accountable for their actions," she said, her voice strong and unwavering. "Our loved ones deserve justice."

These narratives showcased the complex emotional landscape faced by survivors—while some found strength in their stories, others navigated the deep scars left by loss and trauma.

Through these personal accounts, Yingst captured the essence of survival amidst crisis. The stories of Amir, Layla, Maria, and Ahmed not only illustrated the resilience of the human spirit but also highlighted the importance of community, compassion, and hope. These narratives became the backbone of Yingst's coverage, reminding viewers that even in the depths of despair, humanity can shine through, and the will to survive can foster connection, healing, and, ultimately, a brighter future.

The Human Toll of the Conflict

The events of October 7th brought not only physical destruction but also immense emotional suffering to those caught in the crossfire. As the violence escalated, the human toll became increasingly evident. Casualty figures soared, with families torn apart and communities devastated. Amidst the chaos, the stories of loss and survival emerged, painting a harrowing picture of the impact of war on human lives.

Casualties and Loss

As the fighting intensified, hospitals quickly became overwhelmed with injured civilians. The toll on healthcare workers was profound, as they faced relentless waves of casualties. Doctors and nurses worked around the clock, often without adequate resources, struggling to save lives while grappling with the emotional weight of each patient they could not save. Each life lost was a reminder of the fragility of existence in a conflict zone.

Families mourned their loved ones in the aftermath, each death leaving a ripple effect of grief. Communities that once thrived were now haunted by empty spaces where neighbors and friends used to gather. The psychological impact of loss created a pervasive atmosphere of despair. Survivors recounted their experiences with raw emotion, revealing how the trauma of losing loved ones shaped their daily lives.

Psychological Impact on Survivors

For many, the psychological scars left by the conflict would take far longer to heal than physical wounds. Survivors often experienced post-traumatic stress disorder (PTSD), anxiety, and depression, making it difficult to find a sense of normalcy. The sounds of explosions and the sights of destruction became haunting reminders of their experiences, often triggering flashbacks.

Children were particularly vulnerable to the emotional toll of the conflict. Young minds struggled to process the violence they witnessed, leading to increased anxiety and behavioral issues. Parents faced the daunting challenge of comforting their children while grappling with their own trauma. The impact of the conflict extended beyond individual suffering, affecting families and communities at large.

A Cycle of Trauma

As the days turned into weeks, the cycle of trauma became evident. Displacement, loss, and ongoing violence created a fertile ground for further emotional suffering. Many families found themselves living in makeshift shelters, struggling to meet basic needs while grappling with the psychological burden of their circumstances. The ongoing uncertainty and fear stifled any sense of hope for the future.

In the face of such overwhelming suffering, support systems often faltered. Aid organizations worked tirelessly to provide assistance, but the sheer scale of the crisis often left many without the help they desperately needed. This compounded the emotional toll on survivors, who felt abandoned and isolated amid the chaos.

Emotional Toll on Journalists

While the human toll of the conflict was profoundly felt by survivors and victims, the emotional impact on journalists covering the events should not be overlooked. Trey Yingst, along with many other correspondents, faced the dual challenge of reporting on the unfolding tragedy while grappling with their own emotional responses to the violence they witnessed.

Witnessing Trauma Firsthand

For journalists like Yingst, each report involved witnessing scenes of unimaginable suffering. They encountered injured civilians, grieving families, and the aftermath of violence, which took a significant toll on their mental well-being. The emotional burden of capturing these narratives while remaining objective created a complex psychological landscape for many correspondents.

Yingst often spoke about the struggle to maintain composure while reporting. "You try to focus on your job, but it's impossible to disconnect from the humanity of what you're seeing," he explained. The weight of each story became a heavy responsibility, and the emotional impact of the events often lingered long after the cameras were turned off.

Burnout and Fatigue

The relentless nature of war reporting can lead to burnout and emotional fatigue. Journalists may find themselves constantly exposed to traumatic events, leading to desensitization or emotional withdrawal. Yingst and his colleagues worked long hours, often under dangerous conditions, while also facing the pressure of meeting deadlines and delivering accurate reports. The demands of the job left little room for self-care, compounding the emotional toll of their experiences.

Many journalists faced the added challenge of being away from their families and support systems, which further exacerbated feelings of isolation. The stress of working in conflict zones without adequate mental health support can lead to long-term psychological consequences, including anxiety, depression, and PTSD.

Navigating Ethical Dilemmas

Journalists also grapple with ethical dilemmas as they report on human suffering. Yingst often found himself questioning how to balance the need for impactful reporting with the dignity of those affected. "It's a fine line," he remarked. "You want to tell their stories, but you also want to respect their privacy and pain." This internal conflict added another layer to the emotional toll of their work.

Many journalists take on the emotional burdens of the stories they cover, feeling a sense of responsibility to advocate for those whose voices have been silenced. This sense of duty can lead to profound emotional distress, as they navigate the complexities of their role in conveying the realities of war.

The Importance of Support Systems

Recognizing the emotional toll of conflict reporting is essential for the well-being of journalists. Support systems, including mental health resources, peer support groups, and organizational policies prioritizing mental health, are critical in helping correspondents process their experiences.

In the wake of the October 7th conflict, discussions surrounding the mental health of journalists gained traction, emphasizing the need for organizations to prioritize the well-being of their staff. By addressing the emotional toll of war reporting, the industry can create a more supportive environment for those on the front lines, ensuring they have the resources needed to cope with the challenges of their profession.

The emotional toll of the October 7th conflict extended far beyond the immediate casualties. Survivors faced profound grief, trauma, and challenges in rebuilding their lives, while journalists like Trey Yingst navigated their emotional responses to the violence they reported. The interconnectedness of these experiences serves as a reminder of the far-reaching impact of war, affecting not only those directly involved but also those dedicated to sharing their stories with the world.

The Psychological Impact on Trey Yingst

As a war correspondent, Trey Yingst found himself deeply affected by the events he witnessed on October 7th. The psychological impact of covering such a traumatic and chaotic situation can be profound, leaving a lasting imprint on even the most seasoned journalists. Yingst often reflected on the emotional toll of reporting from the front lines, noting how each story shaped his perspective on both the conflict and humanity.

Emotional Exhaustion

The intensity of the situation took a significant emotional toll on Yingst. The constant barrage of violence and suffering forced him to confront the raw reality of war daily. "I remember feeling drained after a long day of reporting," he recounted. "Every story I covered weighed heavily on my heart, and it became increasingly difficult to process everything." This emotional exhaustion is a common experience for journalists in conflict zones, as they are frequently exposed to traumatic events without adequate time for recovery.

Yingst's emotional burden was compounded by the responsibility he felt to accurately convey the stories of those affected by the conflict. "I wanted to do justice to their experiences, but the weight of their suffering was immense," he explained. This sense of responsibility can lead to feelings of guilt and helplessness when reporters are unable to fully capture the gravity of the situations they witness.

Internal Conflict

Yingst also grappled with an internal conflict about his role as a journalist. While he aimed to provide an accurate portrayal of the events unfolding around him, he often found it challenging to remain detached from the emotional realities of the conflict. "You want to tell the truth, but it's impossible not to be affected by what you see," he shared. This struggle to balance emotional engagement with professional objectivity can create an overwhelming psychological burden for correspondents.

Coping Mechanisms

To cope with the psychological impact of his experiences, Yingst relied on various strategies. He emphasized the importance of connecting with fellow journalists, who understood the unique challenges of reporting in conflict zones. "Talking to my colleagues helped," he noted. "We shared our experiences and supported each other through the tough moments."

Additionally, Yingst made a conscious effort to take breaks when possible, allowing himself time to step back from the intensity of his work. Whether through brief moments of solitude or engaging in light-hearted conversations, these coping mechanisms played a crucial role in maintaining his mental well-being amidst the chaos.

The Burden of Reporting in Real-Time

The real-time nature of news reporting, especially in conflict situations, presents unique challenges and burdens for journalists like Trey Yingst. In the age of instant communication, the pressure to deliver timely and accurate updates can be immense, often at the expense of their mental health.

Pressure to Perform

Yingst often faced the pressure of delivering live updates while dealing with the chaos around him. The need to report quickly meant that there was little time for reflection or emotional processing. "When you're on air, you have to focus on delivering the news, but inside, you're dealing with the weight of what's happening," he shared. This pressure to perform can exacerbate the emotional strain on journalists, forcing them to prioritize their roles as reporters over their well-being.

The immediacy of news reporting also creates a sense of urgency that can lead to ethical dilemmas. Yingst reflected on the difficult decisions he had to make regarding what to report and when. "Sometimes, you're faced with the choice of broadcasting a traumatic moment or holding back out of respect for those involved," he explained. Navigating these choices adds another layer of complexity to the emotional burden of reporting.

Impact on Personal Life

The demands of real-time reporting can spill over into journalists' personal lives. Yingst, like many correspondents, often found it challenging to disconnect from work, leading to difficulties in maintaining relationships and personal well-being. "When you're in the field, it's hard to turn off your journalist instincts," he admitted. This inability to fully engage in personal life can contribute to feelings of isolation and disconnection from loved ones.

Finding Balance

Despite the burdens of real-time reporting, Yingst emphasized the importance of finding balance. He acknowledged the necessity of taking breaks and engaging in activities that foster personal well-being. "It's essential to recharge and step away from the news cycle when you can," he advised, recognizing the importance of self-care in sustaining long-term mental health.

Moreover, Yingst highlighted the need for media organizations to prioritize the mental health of their journalists. "There should be resources available to help reporters cope with the psychological impacts of their work," he stated, advocating for greater awareness and support within the industry.

THE GLOBAL REACTION

The events of October 7th sent shockwaves far beyond the immediate conflict zone, sparking a wave of responses from governments, organizations, and citizens across the globe. As news of the violence spread, the world watched closely, with political leaders, international institutions, and the public reacting in different ways. The global reaction to the conflict was a mixture of political maneuvering, diplomatic statements, and humanitarian concerns, highlighting the interconnectedness of today's world and the widespread impact of regional conflicts on the global stage.

How the World Responded to October 7th

The international response to the events of October 7th was immediate and multifaceted, reflecting the complexity of global geopolitics. Governments condemned the violence, some offering diplomatic solutions, while others took a more cautious approach, mindful of the fragile balance in the region. International organizations, human rights groups, and relief agencies also sprang into action, calling for peace and providing aid to those affected. Public demonstrations in various parts of the world echoed calls for justice, highlighting the shared sense of outrage and solidarity that transcended borders.

Political Reactions

Western Governments

The reaction from Western governments was swift, with many leaders expressing concern over the outbreak of violence and calling for an immediate ceasefire. The United States, in particular, played a pivotal role, with statements from the White House condemning the escalation of conflict. President Joe Biden addressed the situation publicly, urging restraint and emphasizing the importance of a diplomatic solution. "The violence must stop," Biden stated in a televised address. "We are working with our allies to de-escalate the situation and bring about a peaceful resolution."

European governments echoed similar sentiments, with leaders from France, the United Kingdom, and Germany condemning the attacks and stressing the need for humanitarian aid. French President Emmanuel Macron called for an emergency meeting of the United Nations Security Council to discuss the situation, while the UK Foreign Office dispatched diplomats to the region to assess the needs of those affected.

At the same time, many Western nations faced internal pressure from their citizens, who were demanding a more robust response to the crisis. Protests erupted in major cities, with demonstrators calling for greater involvement in mediating peace efforts. Governments were forced to balance their diplomatic interests with the growing public outcry for action, leading to a delicate political dance on the world stage.

Middle Eastern Governments

The response from Middle Eastern governments was more divided, reflecting the region's complex political landscape. Some countries, such as Saudi Arabia and the United Arab Emirates, called for calm and emphasized the importance of regional stability. Saudi Arabia, in particular, used its position as a regional power to advocate for dialogue, with Crown Prince Mohammed bin Salman issuing a statement urging all parties to refrain from further escalation. "We must seek peaceful solutions through diplomacy and negotiations," he remarked, calling for an end to the violence.

On the other hand, other regional powers reacted with a more assertive tone. Iran, long a player in regional geopolitics, expressed support for one side of the conflict, further heightening tensions. Iranian officials condemned what they viewed as foreign interference in the region, positioning themselves as defenders of certain groups involved in the fighting. This polarized response from regional actors added another layer of complexity to the conflict, as longstanding rivalries and alliances came to the forefront.

United Nations and International Bodies

International organizations, led by the United Nations, responded quickly, with calls for a ceasefire and increased humanitarian aid. The UN Secretary-General, António Guterres, expressed deep concern over the escalation of violence, urging all parties to prioritize the safety of civilians. "The protection of human lives must be the priority," Guterres said in a statement, calling on the international community to step up efforts to mediate peace and provide aid to those in need.

The UN Security Council convened an emergency session, where member states debated potential resolutions to the conflict. While there was broad agreement on the need for peace, political differences between major powers, such as the United States, Russia, and China, complicated efforts to reach a consensus on actionable steps. Nevertheless, the session underscored the importance of multilateral efforts to address the crisis and the global community's commitment to preventing further bloodshed.

Human Rights Organizations

Human rights organizations also played a critical role in shaping the global reaction to October 7th. Groups such as Amnesty International and Human Rights Watch issued reports documenting the violence, with a focus on civilian casualties and potential war crimes. These organizations called for independent investigations into the events and demanded that those responsible for violations of international law be held accountable.

Their reports, widely covered by global media outlets, further fueled public outrage and increased pressure on governments to act. Human rights advocates emphasized the need for immediate access to humanitarian corridors and the protection of civilians, as well as accountability mechanisms to ensure justice for victims.

Public Protests and Global Solidarity

Around the world, public demonstrations erupted in response to the violence. In cities from New York to Berlin, people took to the streets, holding signs and chanting slogans calling for an end to the conflict. Many of these protests were organized by activist groups, human rights organizations, and members of the diaspora, who were directly affected by the events or felt a deep sense of solidarity with the victims.

Social media platforms played a key role in mobilizing these protests, with hashtags and viral campaigns drawing attention to the crisis and amplifying calls for action. The global solidarity movement highlighted the interconnected nature of modern conflicts and the ability of people across the world to unite in support of justice and peace.

Media Coverage from Different Regions

The media coverage of the events on October 7th varied significantly depending on the region, reflecting diverse political landscapes, cultural perspectives, and media freedom levels. The story dominated global headlines, but the narratives and focus points differed across regions, shaping public perception and government responses.

Western Media

In Western media, particularly in outlets from the United States and Europe, the coverage was immediate and intense, with a focus on the humanitarian crisis and political implications of the conflict. Major networks like CNN, BBC, and The New York Times provided continuous updates, featuring live reports from correspondents on the ground. Journalists like Trey Yingst were pivotal in bringing real-time accounts to audiences, offering a raw and unfiltered view of the violence.

Western media often framed the conflict within the broader context of regional instability and global geopolitical power dynamics. Analysts and commentators debated the role of Western governments in either mitigating or exacerbating tensions, with calls for increased diplomatic efforts. Human interest stories also received considerable attention, with profiles on survivors, victims, and those displaced by the violence.

Middle Eastern Media

In contrast, media outlets in the Middle East offered a more nuanced and regionally-focused portrayal of the conflict. Channels like Al Jazeera and Al Arabiya emphasized the historical and political roots of the violence, often providing a platform for regional actors and experts to discuss the situation. The narrative in many Middle Eastern outlets was shaped by longstanding political alignments and rivalries, with coverage often reflecting the perspectives of the countries in which these outlets were based.

For example, Al Jazeera's coverage focused on the impact of the conflict on the broader Middle East, offering in-depth analysis of how the violence could shift regional power dynamics. The outlet also highlighted the humanitarian toll on civilians, calling for immediate international intervention and emphasizing the need for peace talks.

In more tightly controlled media environments, such as in Iran and some Gulf states, the coverage was filtered through the lens of national interests. State-sponsored outlets aligned their narratives with government positions, emphasizing solidarity with allied factions and often casting blame on foreign interference for exacerbating the situation.

Asian Media

Asian media outlets, including those in China, Japan, and India, provided coverage that focused more on the international repercussions of the conflict rather than the internal dynamics. For instance, Chinese state media took a cautious approach, discussing the conflict in the context of international law and the importance of maintaining regional stability. Coverage highlighted China's official stance of non-intervention, emphasizing diplomatic solutions and urging global powers to refrain from escalating tensions.

Indian media, on the other hand, focused on the potential impact of the conflict on energy supplies and global markets, given the region's significance to India's economy. Reports in Indian outlets also examined the role of international powers like the United States and Russia in the conflict, analyzing how their actions might influence India's foreign policy and its relations with the Middle East.

African and Latin American Media

In African and Latin American media, the coverage was less prominent but still significant, often framed through the lens of global solidarity and the broader implications of the conflict on international peace efforts. South African media, for example, emphasized calls for a peaceful resolution and echoed the sentiment that the violence could further destabilize already fragile regions.

In Latin America, news outlets in countries like Brazil and Argentina reported on the humanitarian aspect of the conflict, with a focus on the role of international organizations such as the United Nations in addressing the crisis. Coverage in these regions often stressed the importance of global cooperation and solidarity, reflecting the distance of these regions from the direct geopolitical consequences but their shared concern over international peace.

The Impact on International Relations

The events of October 7th had profound and far-reaching consequences for international relations, altering diplomatic dynamics and reshaping alliances. The immediate fallout from the conflict was felt in both bilateral and multilateral relations, as countries grappled with how to respond to the crisis without further escalating tensions.

Diplomatic Tensions and Alliances

One of the most notable impacts of the conflict was the strain it placed on diplomatic relationships. The United States and its European allies found themselves at the forefront of international efforts to de-escalate the violence, with many countries emphasizing the need for a coordinated diplomatic response. However, these efforts were often complicated by the involvement of regional powers with competing interests.

For example, the relationship between the United States and Iran, already fraught with tension, became even more strained as each side took opposing stances on the conflict. Iran's support for certain groups involved in the violence led to heightened rhetoric from Washington, with U.S. officials calling for increased sanctions and diplomatic pressure. This further polarized the region, making it more difficult to broker peace.

Meanwhile, Russia and China maintained a more neutral stance, calling for restraint and dialogue but avoiding direct intervention. Both countries were careful to protect their interests in the region, particularly in terms of energy and trade, while navigating the delicate balance between supporting international law and maintaining their alliances.

Shifting Regional Power Dynamics

The conflict also altered the power dynamics within the Middle East itself. Saudi Arabia, long seen as a stabilizing force in the region, found itself in a delicate position, balancing its role as a peacemaker with its strategic alliances. Crown Prince Mohammed bin Salman's calls for calm and dialogue highlighted Saudi Arabia's desire to avoid being drawn into a broader regional conflict, especially as it seeks to focus on domestic reforms and economic diversification under Vision 2030.

At the same time, Turkey and Qatar, both key players in the region, sought to position themselves as mediators in the conflict, offering to host peace talks and facilitate negotiations. Their involvement underscored the shifting alliances in the region, as countries jostled for influence and sought to secure their own strategic interests.

Global Economic and Security Implications

The ripple effects of the conflict were felt globally, particularly in terms of economic and security concerns. The volatility in the region raised fears of disruptions to global energy supplies, particularly in Europe and Asia, where dependence on Middle Eastern oil and gas remains significant. The rise in oil prices in the aftermath of the conflict had a direct impact on global markets, exacerbating existing economic challenges in the wake of the pandemic.

In terms of security, the conflict heightened concerns about the proliferation of violence beyond the region, with many countries stepping up their counterterrorism efforts. Western governments, in particular, were wary of the potential for extremist groups to exploit the instability, leading to increased intelligence-sharing and security cooperation among international partners.

Humanitarian Diplomacy

On the diplomatic front, the humanitarian crisis resulting from the conflict became a central focus of international relations. Countries around the world pledged aid and support for those affected by the violence, with many governments dispatching humanitarian missions to the region. The United Nations, alongside various non-governmental organizations, worked to ensure that humanitarian corridors were established to deliver food, medical supplies, and shelter to displaced populations.

The global response to the humanitarian crisis demonstrated the ability of the international community to unite in the face of tragedy, even as political disagreements persisted. However, the scale of the crisis also underscored the need for long-term solutions to address the root causes of the conflict and prevent future violence.

Diplomatic Consequences

The diplomatic consequences of the events of October 7th were far-reaching, impacting both regional and international relations. Countries directly involved in the conflict saw their diplomatic ties tested, while global powers and international organizations were drawn into the delicate task of mediation. The fallout from the violence prompted shifts in alliances, strained old relationships, and in some cases, opened the door to new diplomatic efforts aimed at peacekeeping and rebuilding.

Strained Relationships and Realignments

One of the most immediate diplomatic consequences of the conflict was the strain it placed on relationships between countries with opposing interests in the region. For instance, the already fragile relationship between the United States and Iran reached new levels of hostility, with Washington accusing Tehran of fueling the violence through its regional proxies. The conflict exacerbated long-standing tensions, making diplomatic negotiations on other issues, such as nuclear talks, even more difficult.

Similarly, the conflict tested the solidarity of alliances within the Arab world. While countries like Saudi Arabia called for peace and emphasized dialogue, other regional players with vested interests in the conflict took more aggressive stances. This led to subtle realignments within the Middle East, as nations reconsidered their strategic alliances in light of the conflict's aftermath.

Increased Diplomatic Pressure on Global Powers

Global powers, particularly the United States, Russia, and China, faced increased diplomatic pressure to intervene and mediate the conflict. Each of these countries had its own interests in the region, and the violence forced them to navigate a complex web of political alliances. The United States, already deeply involved in Middle Eastern affairs, was expected to take the lead in de-escalating tensions, which placed immense pressure on American diplomats to balance domestic and international expectations.

Russia and China, while less directly involved, also faced diplomatic challenges. Russia, with its close ties to some factions in the region, found itself walking a tightrope between supporting its allies and avoiding direct confrontation with Western powers. China, on the other hand, took a more neutral stance, advocating for stability and promoting its vision of non-interference in regional conflicts, while keeping a close eye on how the violence could affect its energy interests.

New Diplomatic Initiatives

Despite the tension, the crisis also opened the door for new diplomatic initiatives. Several countries, including Turkey and Qatar, positioned themselves as potential mediators, offering to host peace talks and facilitate negotiations. These efforts highlighted the possibility of new diplomatic partnerships emerging from the chaos, with regional actors looking to take on more significant roles in conflict resolution.

International organizations like the United Nations and the European Union also ramped up their diplomatic efforts. The UN Security Council, although divided in its response, continued to push for a ceasefire and the establishment of humanitarian corridors. The European Union, grappling with the humanitarian fallout of the crisis, emphasized diplomacy and worked to bring key players to the negotiating table.

Long-Term Changes in Policy

The events of October 7th did not just spark immediate diplomatic consequences; they also triggered long-term changes in national and international policies. Governments around the world began reassessing their foreign policies in light of the conflict, and many countries implemented strategic shifts to better prepare for similar crises in the future.

Reevaluation of Military and Defense Strategies

One of the most significant long-term policy changes was the reevaluation of military and defense strategies, particularly in countries directly affected by the conflict. Middle Eastern nations, especially those near the conflict zone, bolstered their defense systems and reviewed their military preparedness. Some countries increased military spending, modernized their forces, and formed new defense alliances to ensure they could respond more effectively to future regional instability.

In the West, particularly in the United States and Europe, military and intelligence agencies reassessed their roles in the region. The events of October 7th served as a stark reminder of the potential for sudden, large-scale conflict in volatile regions, prompting discussions about the future of military deployments and alliances in the Middle East. NATO, for example, conducted reviews of its presence in the region and considered how it could contribute to preventing further escalations.

Energy and Economic Policies

The impact of the conflict on global energy markets forced many countries, particularly those reliant on Middle Eastern oil and gas, to rethink their energy policies. The sudden spike in oil prices that followed the violence highlighted the vulnerabilities of global energy supplies and the need for diversification.

Several countries in Europe and Asia accelerated their efforts to reduce dependence on Middle Eastern energy sources, investing more heavily in renewable energy, alternative suppliers, and strategic reserves. The conflict also reignited discussions on energy security and the importance of protecting critical infrastructure, such as oil pipelines and refineries, from potential disruptions.

Humanitarian and Refugee Policies

The humanitarian crisis resulting from the conflict had lasting effects on international policies related to refugees and displaced persons. As the violence created waves of refugees fleeing the region, countries in Europe, the Middle East, and beyond were forced to reconsider their refugee policies.

Many nations faced internal debates about how to handle the influx of refugees, balancing humanitarian responsibilities with domestic political pressures. The crisis prompted some countries to strengthen their border controls and tighten immigration policies, while others increased their refugee quotas and provided additional resources for humanitarian aid.

International organizations, such as the UN Refugee Agency (UNHCR), pushed for long-term solutions to address the root causes of displacement and called for more robust international frameworks to manage refugee crises. The conflict also underscored the importance of building resilient systems to support displaced populations, both in the immediate aftermath of violence and in the long term.

Shift Toward Diplomacy and Peacebuilding

One of the most notable long-term changes was a renewed emphasis on diplomacy and peacebuilding as essential components of international relations. The October 7th conflict, with its devastating human toll, prompted governments and international organizations to prioritize conflict prevention and resolution in their foreign policies.

Countries invested more in diplomatic initiatives aimed at addressing the underlying causes of regional conflicts, such as poverty, political instability, and religious tensions. Many governments also increased their funding for peacebuilding programs and supported international efforts to foster dialogue and reconciliation in conflict-prone regions.

This shift towards diplomacy, while not a panacea for all conflicts, represented a recognition that military solutions alone were insufficient to bring lasting peace. As the international community reflected on the lessons of October 7th, there was a growing consensus that sustained diplomatic engagement, combined with humanitarian support, was crucial for preventing future crises.

THE AFTERMATH—A CHANGED LANDSCAPE

Efforts to Rebuild Post-Conflict

In the wake of the violence on October 7th, the task of rebuilding the affected areas became a monumental challenge. The physical destruction caused by the conflict left entire neighborhoods, cities, and regions in ruins, and the social fabric of communities was severely damaged. Rebuilding in a post-conflict landscape required a multifaceted approach, combining infrastructure reconstruction, economic recovery, and efforts to promote reconciliation among fractured communities.

Rebuilding Infrastructure

One of the most immediate needs was the reconstruction of essential infrastructure—homes, schools, hospitals, roads, and utilities—many of which had been destroyed or severely damaged in the fighting. International aid organizations, governments, and non-governmental organizations (NGOs) mobilized quickly to begin the process of rebuilding. Efforts focused on providing immediate relief, such as temporary shelters, food, and medical aid, followed by long-term rebuilding plans.

Countries from around the world pledged financial aid to support these rebuilding efforts, with major contributions from the United Nations, the European Union, and wealthy Middle Eastern nations. Reconstruction required not only rebuilding physical structures but also restoring essential services like water, electricity, and sanitation, which were critical to bringing communities back to life.

In addition, local governments had to address the massive displacement caused by the conflict. Thousands, if not millions, of people had been forced to flee their homes during the violence, and resettling them in safe and stable environments became a priority. International organizations worked closely with local authorities to establish safe zones and create long-term housing solutions for displaced populations.

Economic Recovery

The conflict had devastated local economies, leaving businesses destroyed, jobs lost, and trade disrupted. As the region began to recover, rebuilding the economy was just as important as reconstructing physical infrastructure. The economic impact of the violence was felt both locally and globally, with disruptions to trade routes and the destruction of vital industries, such as agriculture, manufacturing, and tourism.

Post-conflict recovery plans included creating job opportunities for those displaced by the conflict and those whose livelihoods had been destroyed. This involved a focus on stimulating local economies by investing in small businesses, providing micro-loans, and encouraging foreign investment. International agencies like the World Bank and International Monetary Fund (IMF) played a key role in supporting these recovery efforts, offering loans and grants to help kick-start economic growth in affected areas.

To aid in the long-term recovery, governments also introduced policies to rebuild key industries, including agriculture and manufacturing, and supported infrastructure projects that would improve transportation and trade networks, facilitating economic revival. Regional cooperation also became a focus, as neighboring countries offered assistance in trade and infrastructure rebuilding efforts.

Reconciliation and Healing

Reconstruction efforts were not limited to physical rebuilding and economic recovery. The emotional and psychological toll of the conflict left deep scars on communities, with people struggling to come to terms with the loss of loved ones, homes, and livelihoods. Reconciliation and healing efforts became a critical component of the post-conflict recovery process, addressing the social divisions and trauma that had been exacerbated by the violence.

Promoting Dialogue and Reconciliation

In the aftermath of the conflict, there was a clear need for efforts to foster dialogue and promote reconciliation between the various groups affected by the violence. Communities that had been divided along ethnic, religious, or political lines needed help in rebuilding trust and relationships. Governments, NGOs, and peacebuilding organizations played key roles in facilitating discussions between opposing groups, encouraging communication and understanding.

Truth and reconciliation commissions, similar to those seen in other post-conflict regions, were established to investigate and document the atrocities committed during the violence. These commissions provided a platform for victims to share their stories and seek justice, while also allowing perpetrators to be held accountable for their actions. This process of truth-telling was seen as an essential step in healing the deep wounds caused by the conflict.

Psychological Support and Mental Health

The psychological toll of the conflict was immense, affecting not only the survivors but also the journalists, aid workers, and military personnel who had witnessed the atrocities firsthand. Mental health services were urgently needed to address the widespread trauma experienced by individuals and communities.

International organizations, along with local health services, provided psychological support, counseling, and trauma care to those affected by the violence. Specialized programs were developed to help children who had been displaced or who had lost family members during the conflict. These programs aimed to provide emotional support and stability, helping children return to school and regain a sense of normalcy.

In addition, community-based healing initiatives were launched to address the collective trauma experienced by entire populations. These initiatives focused on creating safe spaces for people to share their experiences, express their grief, and begin the process of healing. Art therapy, group counseling, and memorial services were some of the methods used to help communities come together and cope with their shared loss.

The Role of the International Community

The international community played a pivotal role in both the immediate response to the October 7th conflict and the long-term rebuilding efforts that followed. From humanitarian aid to diplomatic interventions, the global response was critical in helping the region recover from the devastating impact of the violence.

Humanitarian Aid and Assistance

International aid poured into the region in the immediate aftermath of the conflict, with countries and organizations sending food, medical supplies, and financial assistance to those in need. The United Nations and the International Red Cross were among the key players in coordinating the global humanitarian response, ensuring that aid reached the most vulnerable populations.

In addition to direct aid, many countries also provided financial support for long-term recovery efforts. This included funding for infrastructure projects, healthcare initiatives, and educational programs aimed at helping children affected by the conflict. The international community's commitment to providing ongoing support was crucial in helping the region rebuild and recover.

Diplomatic and Peacebuilding Efforts

Diplomatically, the conflict spurred renewed efforts to promote peace and stability in the region. International actors, including the United States, European Union, and key Middle Eastern powers, engaged in intensive diplomatic efforts to broker ceasefires, facilitate peace talks, and support reconciliation efforts.

Multilateral organizations, such as the United Nations and the Arab League, also played a key role in promoting dialogue and peacebuilding initiatives. These efforts focused not only on addressing the immediate aftermath of the conflict but also on preventing future violence by tackling the root causes of instability in the region.

The Legacy of October 7th

The events of October 7th left an indelible mark on the region and the world, reshaping political dynamics, altering international relations, and leaving behind a legacy of loss and resilience. As the region continued to rebuild, the lessons learned from the conflict would shape future efforts to prevent violence and promote peace.

The October 7th conflict served as a stark reminder of the fragility of peace in volatile regions and the importance of sustained international engagement in conflict prevention and resolution. The global response to the crisis highlighted the capacity for collective action, even in the face of profound challenges, and underscored the need for long-term solutions that address both the immediate and underlying causes of conflict.

While the road to recovery was long and difficult, the efforts to rebuild and reconcile after October 7th offered hope for a more stable and peaceful future in the region.

Humanitarian Response to the Crisis

The humanitarian response to the October 7th crisis was swift and comprehensive, as international organizations, NGOs, and local authorities rushed to address the immediate needs of those affected. The conflict resulted in widespread devastation, with thousands displaced, hundreds injured, and communities left in dire need of basic necessities such as food, clean water, shelter, and medical care.

Emergency Relief Efforts

One of the first responses to the crisis came in the form of emergency relief, coordinated by international organizations like the United Nations (UN), the Red Cross, and Médecins Sans Frontières (Doctors Without Borders). These groups quickly deployed teams to the hardest-hit areas, setting up emergency camps and medical facilities. Their immediate focus was on saving lives by providing urgent medical assistance to those injured during the conflict and addressing the spread of disease in areas with compromised sanitation.

Humanitarian airlifts and convoys delivered essential supplies such as food, water, and blankets to affected regions. Governments from around the world also sent financial aid and support in the form of medical teams, engineers, and logistics experts. Countries like the United States,

Canada, and many European nations contributed millions of dollars in humanitarian assistance to support these efforts, while Middle Eastern countries pledged additional financial aid to help stabilize the region.

Support for Displaced Populations

The violence had forced thousands of people to flee their homes, creating a major refugee crisis. Temporary shelters were established in neighboring regions and countries, but many displaced families were left living in overcrowded camps with limited access to resources. As the refugee crisis deepened, international efforts to provide support intensified. The UN Refugee Agency (UNHCR) worked closely with local governments to establish longer-term shelters and ensure that refugees had access to healthcare, education, and psychosocial support.

Reintegration and resettlement programs were also launched, although the massive scale of displacement posed significant challenges. Some countries offered asylum to refugees, while others worked to ensure that those displaced within the region received the care and support they needed to survive in the post-conflict environment.

Long-Term Humanitarian Projects

As the situation transitioned from emergency relief to long-term recovery, humanitarian organizations shifted their focus to rebuilding and development efforts. Infrastructure projects aimed at repairing roads, schools, and hospitals became a priority, while development agencies worked to restore access to clean water and electricity.

Education programs were also initiated to help displaced children resume their studies, and community rehabilitation programs sought to address the long-term psychological impacts of the conflict. Organizations like the International Rescue Committee (IRC) played a significant role in ensuring that mental health and trauma support services were available to survivors, particularly for children who had experienced the horrors of war.

How Trey Yingst Reflected on the Events

Trey Yingst, who covered the October 7th conflict with a front-row view of the chaos, often reflected on the profound impact of these events in his reporting and personal interviews. His insights captured the raw human emotions, political complexities, and long-lasting effects of the crisis, offering a window into the broader realities of modern warfare and journalism.

Witnessing the Human Suffering

Yingst often emphasized the emotional toll of witnessing human suffering on such a massive scale. As a war correspondent, he had been to many conflict zones, but the scale and intensity of the October 7th events were different. He spoke candidly about the helplessness he felt as he documented the struggles of civilians, many of whom had lost everything in a matter of hours. His reflections frequently touched on the resilience of the people he encountered, as well as their deep suffering and trauma.

He shared stories of families torn apart, communities reduced to rubble, and children left orphaned by the violence. In interviews, Yingst described how those personal encounters had stayed with him long after the cameras were turned off, and how difficult it was to distance himself emotionally from the stories he reported.

The Moral Dilemmas of War Reporting

Throughout his coverage, Yingst also reflected on the moral dilemmas that war reporters face. Reporting in real time from the ground presented constant challenges—not just the physical dangers of being in a war zone but also the ethical responsibility of conveying the truth amidst chaos and propaganda.

He spoke about the struggle to remain objective while covering the deeply personal stories of loss and survival, as well as the pressure to balance urgency with accuracy in reporting such a fast-moving and violent conflict. Yingst also discussed the responsibility that comes with amplifying the voices of those affected, ensuring that their stories are not forgotten or misrepresented.

Impact on His Own Mental Health

Trey Yingst has been open about the psychological toll that covering such events has taken on him personally. He often reflected on the emotional and mental strain of being constantly exposed to scenes of death, destruction, and human suffering. The October 7th conflict, in particular, had a profound impact on him, not just as a journalist but as a human being.

In interviews following the conflict, Yingst admitted that his experience left him with a heavy emotional burden. He shared how difficult it was to process the trauma and horror of what he had witnessed, and how the mental health struggles faced by war correspondents often go unspoken. Yingst became a vocal advocate for better mental health support for journalists, emphasizing the need for self-care and professional help in the aftermath of such traumatic events.

The Legacy of His Coverage

In the months and years that followed, Trey Yingst's reporting on the October 7th conflict became a reference point for understanding the human cost of war. His reflections on the events provided not just a journalistic account but a deeply personal and emotional narrative that captured the essence of the conflict. His interviews and reports highlighted the broader implications of the violence, from the humanitarian crises to the political and diplomatic fallout that would continue to shape the region for years to come.

Through his coverage, Yingst provided a voice for the voiceless, ensuring that the stories of the survivors, victims, and communities affected by the October 7th conflict were heard around the world. His reflections remain a vital part of the historical record of those tragic events.

His Post-Conflict Coverage

After the immediate chaos of October 7th subsided, Trey Yingst's post-conflict coverage continued to offer critical insights into the long-term effects of the conflict. As a war correspondent, he understood that the story didn't end when the violence stopped; the real work of recovery, healing, and rebuilding was just beginning. Yingst stayed on the ground in the aftermath, documenting the lingering humanitarian crisis, the ongoing political struggles, and the complex process of rebuilding shattered communities.

His reporting during this period shifted focus from the battlefield to the human side of the post-conflict recovery. Yingst highlighted the efforts of international aid organizations trying to deliver relief in devastated areas, the displaced families seeking shelter and stability, and the psychological scars left on survivors. He conducted interviews with local leaders, aid workers, and ordinary civilians who were trying to make sense of their new reality and figure out how to move forward in the wake of unimaginable loss.

By staying on the ground, Yingst was able to bring attention to stories that might otherwise have been overlooked in the global media, which tends to move on once the most dramatic moments of conflict are over.

His post-conflict coverage emphasized that even when the cameras turned away, the suffering and challenges for those on the ground persisted. Through his detailed reporting, Yingst continued to shine a light on the lasting consequences of war, reminding the world that rebuilding was a slow, difficult process that required sustained attention and effort.

Long-Term Impact on His Career

The events of October 7th and the subsequent conflict marked a turning point in Trey Yingst's career. Already a well-respected war correspondent, his coverage of this event cemented his reputation as one of the most fearless and empathetic journalists working in conflict zones. The experience pushed him to new levels of professional and personal growth, expanding his role from reporter to a storyteller who deeply engaged with the human cost of conflict.

Following October 7th, Yingst became more involved in discussions about the ethical and emotional burdens of war reporting. He often spoke publicly about the challenges faced by journalists covering conflict, advocating for mental health support and safety protocols for reporters working in dangerous environments. His work also raised awareness about the impact that repeated exposure to trauma can have on journalists, leading him to become a vocal advocate for providing resources to support the mental well-being of those on the front lines of reporting.

Career-wise, his in-depth coverage of the conflict opened up new opportunities. News networks and organizations recognized the value of his on-the-ground insights and empathetic storytelling. His work was not only broadcast widely but also cited in academic studies and humanitarian reports. Yingst began to be seen as a key voice in discussions about media ethics, the role of journalism in conflict zones, and the importance of keeping human stories at the forefront of reporting.

As a result of his experiences, Trey Yingst's career evolved from being just a war correspondent to becoming a figure who also spoke on the broader implications of conflict journalism, trauma, and the importance of resilience in both the profession and the human spirit. The long-term impact of October 7th was not just felt in his reporting, but also in how it shaped the direction of his career, giving him a platform to speak out on issues that he had experienced firsthand.

THE POWER OF JOURNALISM IN CONFLICT ZONES

The Role of War Correspondents

War correspondents play a vital role in bringing the realities of conflict to the attention of the world. Operating in some of the most dangerous and volatile environments, they serve as the eyes and ears of the global community, reporting on events that are often underreported or misrepresented. These journalists face significant personal risks, but their work is crucial in shaping the public's understanding of conflicts and their impact on civilians, political structures, and the future of entire regions.

In conflict zones, correspondents not only report on the immediate violence but also delve into the underlying causes of unrest, the humanitarian consequences, and the efforts at peace and reconstruction. Their role is to capture the truth, even when the truth is messy, painful, and dangerous. This often means confronting their own emotional and moral challenges as they witness some of humanity's darkest moments.

Through their reporting, war correspondents act as mediators between the conflict zone and the rest of the world. They provide a direct link to the experiences of those affected by war, and they hold governments, armed groups, and international bodies accountable by exposing atrocities and human rights abuses. Their work can shape public opinion, influence international policy, and, in some cases, help to resolve conflicts or drive humanitarian aid to where it is most needed.

How Journalists Shape the Narrative

Journalists in conflict zones have a profound ability to shape the narrative surrounding a conflict. The way they frame stories, select their sources, and highlight certain aspects of the war can influence how the global audience perceives both the conflict itself and the people involved. War correspondents make choices—often in real time—about what to show, who to interview, and which angles to explore, and these decisions can have far-reaching consequences.

For instance, how a journalist chooses to report on civilian casualties can shift the tone of international discourse. Focusing on the human cost of war—interviewing survivors, highlighting the destruction of homes and schools, and documenting the experiences of displaced families—can generate empathy and pressure governments or international bodies to intervene. On the other hand, focusing on military strategies, weaponry, or geopolitical gamesmanship might shift attention toward the more impersonal, strategic aspects of war.

War correspondents like Trey Yingst, who emphasize the human element in their stories, often influence how conflicts are remembered and understood long after the fighting ends. By giving a voice to those who are most affected—civilians, refugees, aid workers—these journalists ensure that the human dimension of war is not lost in the political and military analysis. This storytelling helps keep the focus on the broader implications of conflict, such as its long-term effects on communities and individuals, which can otherwise be overshadowed by short-term military or political victories.

Furthermore, journalists who report on both sides of a conflict provide a more nuanced understanding of the situation, challenging simplistic or one-sided narratives that may be pushed by political leaders or propaganda machines. In doing so, they help foster a more informed and balanced global discourse, which is crucial for diplomacy and peace-building efforts. Through their work, war correspondents have the power to bring visibility to the invisible and make the global community care about places and people they might otherwise overlook.

Ethical Dilemmas in Reporting

War correspondents, like Trey Yingst, constantly face complex ethical dilemmas in their reporting. These dilemmas often arise in the fast-paced, chaotic environments of conflict zones where journalists must make split-second decisions that can have far-reaching consequences. One of the most significant challenges is the balance between the duty to report the truth and the potential harm that certain information might cause.

For instance, when reporting on sensitive military operations, journalists must consider the risk of inadvertently revealing strategic information that could endanger soldiers or civilians. There is also the ethical question of whether to broadcast images of extreme violence or suffering. While such footage can highlight the brutal reality of war and prompt international intervention, it can also traumatize audiences or exploit the suffering of victims.

Another critical dilemma is the issue of impartiality. War reporters are expected to maintain neutrality, presenting both sides of the conflict objectively. However, in situations where one side is clearly perpetrating atrocities or violating human rights, remaining neutral can feel morally wrong. Journalists must navigate these treacherous waters carefully, ensuring they report facts without allowing their personal emotions or biases to overshadow the truth.

Yingst, like many war correspondents, has spoken about the emotional toll of documenting human suffering and the responsibility that comes with telling these stories. He has grappled with the ethical implications of showing the world the horrors of war while ensuring that the dignity and humanity of those he reports on are respected. Such dilemmas are an inherent part of war journalism, and each decision can have lasting consequences on public perception, international policy, and the lives of those directly affected by conflict.

Trey Yingst's Legacy as a Journalist

Trey Yingst's legacy as a journalist is defined not only by his courage in reporting from some of the world's most dangerous conflict zones but also by his commitment to ethical journalism and his dedication to humanizing the stories of war. His reporting on the events of October 7th and other conflicts around the globe has left an indelible mark on the field of war correspondence, shaping how the world understands and responds to modern warfare.

One of the key elements of Yingst's legacy is his ability to bring attention to the human cost of conflict. While many journalists focus primarily on the political or military dimensions of war, Yingst has consistently highlighted the personal stories of those caught in the crossfire—civilians, refugees, and survivors who often go unheard in the broader narrative of war. His interviews with survivors of bombings, displaced families, and aid workers have given a voice to the voiceless, reminding the global audience that war is not just about territory or power; it's about the people whose lives are forever changed.

Yingst's willingness to confront the psychological and emotional impact of war—both on himself and on the people he reports on—also sets him apart. His openness about the mental health struggles faced by war correspondents has brought attention to an often-overlooked aspect of journalism, advocating for better support systems for journalists who operate in such intense, traumatic environments. By speaking openly about the personal toll of war reporting, Yingst has helped destigmatize the mental health challenges faced by many in the profession.

Moreover, his ethical approach to journalism, particularly his careful consideration of the impact his stories might have on those involved, has earned him respect within the journalistic community. He has remained committed to the truth, even when it's uncomfortable or dangerous, and has shown that war correspondents can play a crucial role in not only informing the world but also fostering empathy and understanding in the face of global conflict.

Trey Yingst's legacy will undoubtedly inspire future generations of journalists. His work serves as a reminder of the power of journalism to influence the course of history, shape international relations, and, most importantly, keep the human element at the heart of every story.

His Unique Approach to Storytelling

Trey Yingst's storytelling stands out in the world of war journalism for its deeply personal, human-centered approach. Rather than simply reporting the facts of a conflict, Yingst weaves narratives that focus on the emotional and psychological realities of those living through war. His stories often begin with a single individual's experience—whether it's a mother fleeing with her children, a soldier reflecting on the trauma of battle, or a local aid worker risking their life to help others. These personal accounts draw readers and viewers in, making global conflicts feel more immediate and relatable.

Yingst's unique approach lies in his ability to balance hard-hitting journalism with empathy. He asks questions that reveal the humanity of his subjects, probing not just for facts but for feelings, hopes, and fears. This ability to connect with people on a personal level allows him to uncover layers of the conflict that might otherwise go unnoticed. His storytelling does not shy away from the harsh realities of war, but it also highlights moments of resilience, courage, and even hope amid the devastation.

Moreover, Yingst often employs vivid, sensory details to paint a clear picture of the scenes he is reporting from. Descriptions of the sounds of bombs falling, the smell of burning rubble, or the sight of children playing in the ruins bring his stories to life in a way that engages the audience on an emotional level. This immersive style of storytelling helps the global audience not just understand the conflict but feel it, too. Through his unique narrative techniques, Yingst makes the distant, foreign, and abstract aspects of war seem personal and urgent, fostering a deeper connection between the audience and the stories of those affected by conflict.

The Impact of His Reports on the Global Audience

Trey Yingst's reports have had a profound impact on the global audience, particularly in how people perceive and understand the complexities of war. His ability to humanize the conflict has made his coverage resonate with viewers and readers worldwide, turning abstract geopolitical issues into deeply personal stories that evoke empathy and action.

One of the most significant impacts of Yingst's work is the way it has brought attention to underreported or forgotten crises. His focus on the human side of the story ensures that people don't just see war as a series of statistics or distant political maneuvers but as a series of personal tragedies and triumphs. His reports often shine a light on the voices of those who are rarely heard—refugees, civilians caught in crossfire, local aid workers—and this focus has inspired international responses, from humanitarian aid to political pressure.

Yingst's reports have also played a crucial role in shaping public opinion. His ability to show both the immediate and long-term effects of conflict challenges viewers to think critically about the role of their own governments, international organizations, and global alliances in these crises. The personal stories he shares often create a sense of urgency that prompts action, whether it's through donations to humanitarian organizations or public calls for diplomatic or military interventions.

For many, his work serves as a stark reminder of the ongoing realities of war, even when the headlines have moved on. By continuously reporting from the ground and following up on stories long after the peak of the conflict, Yingst keeps global attention focused on the issues that matter most—helping to prevent the world from forgetting about those still suffering in post-conflict areas.

In sum, the impact of Trey Yingst's reports on the global audience extends beyond just informing people; it touches their emotions, changes their perspectives, and sometimes even moves them to take action. His stories challenge viewers to confront the human cost of conflict and remind the world of its responsibility to those affected by war. Through his empathetic, detailed storytelling, Yingst has built a legacy of journalism that not only informs but also inspires.

CONCLUSION

Reflecting on "The Saturday That Turned Black"

"The Saturday That Turned Black" marked a pivotal moment not only in the history of conflict journalism but also in the broader narrative of modern warfare. October 7th, with its sudden escalation and widespread devastation, served as a reminder of how quickly tensions can ignite into full-blown crises. It also highlighted the role that war correspondents, like Trey Yingst, play in ensuring the world bears witness to these moments in real time. As we reflect on this day, the importance of accurate, empathetic, and responsible journalism becomes even more evident.

For Yingst, October 7th was not just a story of violence but a personal and professional turning point. His coverage of the events—on the ground, in the thick of the chaos—brought raw, unfiltered reality to the world's screens. The images and narratives that emerged from his work reminded us that, behind every headline, there are countless individual stories of loss, survival, and resilience. This day, in particular, underscored the value of journalism in shaping how the world understands conflict and its aftermath.

Lessons Learned from October 7th

One of the most significant lessons from October 7th is the unpredictable nature of conflict. The events of that day developed rapidly, catching even seasoned observers off guard. It serves as a reminder that in regions where tensions simmer, conflict can erupt at any moment, making the presence of journalists on the ground essential for documenting these sudden escalations. The day also taught us about the profound impact that individual voices—survivors, witnesses, and journalists—can have on how the world interprets and reacts to such events.

Another key lesson is the resilience of the human spirit. Despite the horrors of that day, stories of survival and compassion emerged, showcasing the strength of communities in crisis. These stories, amplified through Yingst's reporting, offer a sense of hope even in the darkest times, reminding us that humanity often finds ways to endure and rebuild in the aftermath of destruction.

Finally, the psychological toll on journalists, particularly those covering war and conflict, cannot be overlooked. October 7th reinforced the need for mental health support for journalists who are repeatedly exposed to trauma. The emotional burden of reporting on conflict, especially in real-time, can have lasting effects, making it crucial for the industry to address these issues proactively.

The Continued Importance of Journalism in Crisis Reporting

October 7th reaffirmed the critical role of journalism in crisis reporting. Without reporters like Trey Yingst on the ground, the world might never have fully understood the scale and significance of the events as they unfolded. In a world where misinformation can spread rapidly and the truth is often obscured, the role of journalists in delivering accurate, firsthand accounts is more important than ever.

Journalists serve not only as witnesses to history but also as a bridge between the affected and the rest of the world. They shine a light on the darkest corners of war, ensuring that the stories of those most impacted by conflict are not forgotten. The continued importance of journalism, especially in war zones, lies in its ability to shape the global response— whether that means rallying humanitarian aid, shifting public opinion, or holding those responsible for atrocities accountable.

Trey Yingst's coverage of October 7th demonstrated that, even in the most chaotic and dangerous situations, journalists have the power to make a difference. His work has left a lasting legacy, showing that responsible, empathetic, and courageous reporting can bring clarity to even the most complex and tragic events. As conflicts continue to erupt around the world, the need for dedicated war correspondents like Yingst remains as pressing as ever.

Made in United States
Troutdale, OR
10/12/2024

23686323R00058